Garbage Delight

The poems
were written by
Dennis Lee

The pictures
were drawn by
Frank Newfeld

HarperCollins Publishers Ltd

for Julian and for Hugh Kane

Garbage Delight
Text © Dennis Lee, 1977
Illustrations © Frank Newfeld, 1977
All rights reserved.

Published by HarperCollins Publishers Ltd.

Originally published in 1977 by the Macmillan Company of Canada Ltd.

First published by HarperCollins Publishers Ltd
in this hardcover edition: 2012

HarperCollins Publishers Ltd
2 Bloor Street East, 20th Floor
Toronto, Ontario, Canada
M4W 1A8

www.harpercollins.ca

Library and Archives Canada Cataloguing in Publication

Lee, Dennis, 1939–
Garbage delight : classic edition / Dennis Lee ; Frank
Newfeld, illustrator.

ISBN 978-1-44341-155-4

1. Children's poetry, Canadian (English).
I. Newfeld, Frank, 1928– II. Title.

PS8523.E3G37 2012   jC811'.54   C2012-900845-1

DESIGN: FRANK NEWFELD

Printed and bound in Canada
DWF 9 8 7 6 5 4 3 2 1

Contents

Being Five

I'm not exactly big,
    And I'm not exactly little,
But being Five is best of all
    Because it's in the middle.

A person likes to ride his bike
    Around the block a lot,
And being Five is big enough
    And being Four is not.

And then he likes to settle down
    And suck his thumb a bit,
And being Five is small enough,
    But when you're Six you quit.

I've thought about it in my mind –
    Being Five, I mean –
And why I like it best of all
    Is 'cause it's In Between.

The Moon

I see the moon
And the moon sees me
And nobody sees
As secretly

Unless there's a kid
In Kalamazoo,
Or Mexico,
Or Timbuktu,

Who looks in the sky
At the end of a day,
And he thinks of me
In a friendly way —

'Cause we both lie still
And we watch the moon;
And we haven't met yet
But we might do, soon.

Half Way Dressed

I sometimes sit
    When I'm half way dressed,
With my head in a sweater
    And I feel depressed.

I'm half way out
    And I'm half way in
And my head's nearly through
    But the sweater's gonna win,

'Cause the neck-hole grabs
    Like as if it's glue,
And my ears don't like it,
    And my nose don't, too,

And I can't stand sweaters
    When they grab this way,
And they jump on a kid
    And decide to play.

I'm half way dressed,
    And I'm half way dead,
And I'm half way ready
    To crawl back to bed.

Peter Was a Pilot

Peter was a pilot,

He flew a jumbo jet,

He crashed in Lake Ontario

And got his bottom wet.

Quintin and Griffin

Quintin's sittin' hittin' Griffin,

Griffin's hittin' Quintin too.

If Quintin's quittin' hittin' Griffin,

What will Griffin sit 'n' do?

Bath Song

A biscuit, a basket, a bath in a hat,
An elephant stuck in a tub:
Seize her, and squeeze her, and see if she's fat,
And give her a rub-a-dub-dub.

A biscuit, a basket, a bath in a hat,
An elephant stuck in a spoon:
Seize her, and squeeze her, and see if she's fat,
And give her a ride to the moon.

Skindiver

Wiggle your toenails
    And jiggle your toes:
Skindiver's coming
    To land on your nose.

Wiggle your tummy
    And squiggle your tum:
Skindiver's coming
    To bounce on your bum.

Wiggle your headlight
    And jiggle your head:
Skindiver's coming
    To tuck you to bed.

The Last Cry of the Damp Fly

Bitter batter boop!
I'm swimming in your soup.

Bitter batter bout:
Kindly get me out!

Bitter batter boon:
Not upon your spoon!

Bitter batter bum!
Now I'm in your tum!

A Sasquatch from Saskatchewan

A sasquatch from Saskatchewan

Is chasing me across the lawn.

My friends are going to stare and grin

When they observe the shape I'm in.

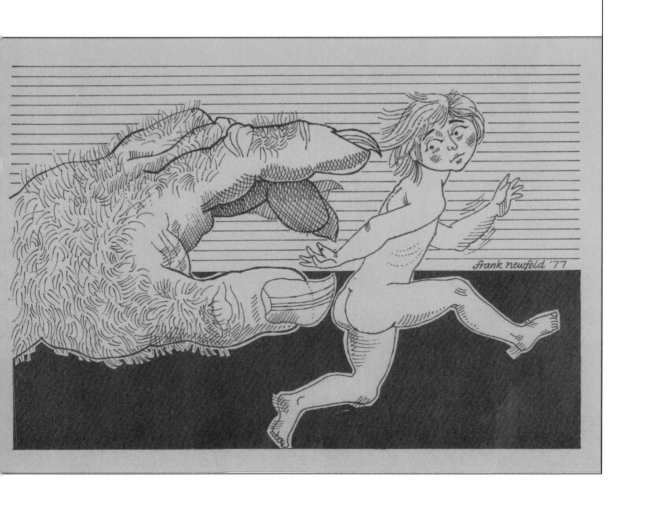

Muffin and Puffin and Murphy and Me

Muffin and Puffin and Murphy and me
Went to Vancouver to swim in the sea.
Muffin went swimming, and swallowed a shark
Puffin saw whales in Stanley Park
Murphy got lost and went bump in the dark
    And I had a strawberry soda.

Muffin and Puffin and Murphy and me
Came back from Vancouver, and back from the sea.
Muffin is puffing from eating the shark
Puffin is huffing from Stanley Park
Murphy is frightened to sleep in the dark
    But I had a strawberry soda!

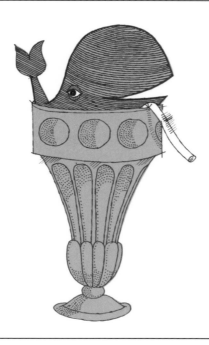

Worm

Some people think a worm is rude,
'Cause he's mostly not in a talkative mood.

And other people think he's dumb,
'Cause he likes you to call, but he doesn't come.

But I've got a worm, and his name is Worm,
And he lives in a jar with a bunch of germs,

And Worm is as smart as a worm can be.
I talk to him and he listens to me:

I tell him the time I fell downstairs
And I teach him the names of my teddy bears

And we both sit still, and I hear the things
That you hear when a worm begins to sing –

About dirt in the yard, and tunnels, and drains,
And having a bath in the grass when it rains.

And we plan about snacks, and not washing your hands
And the letter J. And he understands.

The Aminals

At night the aminals go marching
    Round and round the room.
There's Bigfoot, and McGonigle,
    And Hannah V. Varoom.
And round they march and round they march
    And halt and say, "Beware!"
And all of them are friends of mine
    So none of them are scared.

Now, Bigfoot's kind of squishable,
    The softy of them all;
McGonigle is silly
    'Cause he likes to climb the wall;
And Hannah's pretty big I guess,
    She's maybe six or twelve,
And all of them have shadows that go
    Marching by themselves.

And every shadow makes another
    Shadow right behind.
They're marching on the table-top,
    They're marching up the blind.
And every time they meet they seem to
    All get in the way,
And so they all Beware, and then
    They march the other way.

Round and round the aminals
    Are marching round my room.
There's Bigfoot, and McGonigle,
    And Hannah V. Varoom,
Their shadows, and their shadows'
    Shadows, more and more and more,
Marching like the Mounties round and
    Round the bedroom floor.

The Summerhill Fair

I found a balloon and it went up a tree
I learned how to ride on a pony for free
And I looked at a girl and she knew it was me
    When I went to the Summerhill Fair.

The fishpond was fine, they had monsters and toads
And Dad got a plant and it broke in the road
And I think I remember which pony she rode
    When I went to the Summerhill Fair.

Next year there's a fair at the very same place
I hope I run frontwards and win in the race
And I'll recognize her by the dirt on her face
    When I go to the Summerhill Fair.

McGonigle's Tail

What shall I do with McGonigle's tail?
It came off again, 'cause he swang on the rail.

I'd give it to Bigfoot to tie up the spoons,
But he'd probably use it for catching baboons.

I'd give it to Hannah to put in her bed,
But she'd probably call it Rebecca or Fred.

I'd keep it myself, and I'd put it on too,
But they'd probably say I belonged in the zoo.

It's long and it's off and it can't be For Sale:
What shall I do with McGonigle's tail?

I tried with some glue,
    But the glue wouldn't do:
It squished and it squashed
    And it fell on my shoe.

I tried with a pin
    But it wouldn't stay in:
It bent and it went
    For a sort of a spin.

So I took out some gum,
    And I chewed on it some,
And I plastered it round
    With the end of my thumb –

And McGonigle's tail
    Is as flippy as new,
And it hangs from the rear
    Like it used to do.

And here he is back
    On the banister rail!
And that is the tale
    Of McGonigle's tail.

The Swing

The swing swings up
    And the swing swings down
And the swing swings wishing-wings
    High above town.

And when I go high
    And I feel it sway
I'll hang for a minute
    Or hang for a day

And when I go low
    And I make it whizz
I'll come down forever
    And feel it fizz

But the swing swings up
    And the swing swings down
And the swing swings wishing-wings
    High above town.

Suzy Grew a Moustache

Suzy grew a moustache,
    A moustache,
    A moustache,
Suzy grew a moustache,
    And Polly grew a beard.

Suzy looked peculiar,
    Peculiar,
    Peculiar,
Suzy looked peculiar,
    And Polly looked weird.

Suzy got the garden-shears,
    Garden-shears,
    The garden-shears,
Suzy got the garden-shears
    And Polly got a bomb.

Now Suzy's face is smooth again,
    Smooth again,
    Smooth again,
Suzy's face is smooth again,
    And Polly's face is gone.

Inspector Dogbone Gets His Man

Inspector Dogbone
    Is my name
And catching bad guys
    Is my game.

I catch them hot
    I catch them cold
I catch them when they're
    Nine days old

I catch them here
    I catch them there
I catch them in
    Their underwear

I like to catch them
    By the toes
Or by the moustache
    Or the nose

From Corner Brook
    To Calgary
There's not a cop
    Can copy me

'Cause every time
    I catch a crook
I hang him up
    On a big brass hook –

Yet here I sit
    In the old Don Jail:
Come gather round
    And I'll tell my tale.

One day, as I
    Was walking out,
I caught a bad guy
    By the snout

He robbed a million-
    Dollar bank
I grabbed his snout
    And gave a yank

I grabbed his snoot
    And gave a flick
But then he played
    A bad-guy trick:

His greasy beak
    Was big and tough –
But with a snap
    He bit it off

And just like that
    His smelly schnozz
Had vanished down
    His smelly jaws!

At once I grabbed him
    By the knee:
He ate that too
    And laughed at me

His neck, his arms,
    His back, his feet –
Whatever I seized
    The man would eat

Till all there was
    Was just a mouth –
Which swallowed itself,
    And scampered south.

The case was gone!
    The case was gone!
The nose and the toes
    And the face were gone!

I had no crook
    I had no crime
My mighty brain
    Worked overtime

And figured out
    A mighty plan
For Dogbone always
    Gets his man.

I had no crime
    I had no crook
The only person
    Left to book

Was one whom I
    Had long suspected –
Inspector Dogbone,
    Whom I arrested.

I didn't quake
    I didn't quail
I threw myself
    In the old Don Jail

And here I sit
    Till the end of time,
Easing my soul
    With a Dogbone rhyme,

The victim of
    A bad guy's mouth,
Which swallowed itself
    And scampered south.

But please recall
    As I rot in jail –
Inspector Dogbone
    Didn't fail!

And please remember
    When you can –
Inspector Dogbone
    Got his man!

The Coming of Teddy Bears

The air is quiet
    Round my bed.
The dark is drowsy
    In my head.
The sky's forgetting
    To be red,
And soon I'll be asleep.

A half a million
    Miles away
The silver stars
    Come out to play,
And comb their hair
    And that's OK
And soon I'll be asleep.

And teams of fuzzy
    Teddy bears
Are stumping slowly
    Up the stairs
To rock me in
    Their rocking chairs
And soon I'll be asleep.

The night is shining
    Round my head.
The room is snuggled
    In my bed.
Tomorrow I'll be
    Big they said
And soon I'll be asleep.

The Muddy Puddle

I am sitting
In the middle
Of a rather Muddy
Puddle,
With my bottom
Full of bubbles
And my rubbers
Full of Mud,

While my jacket
And my sweater
Go on slowly
Getting wetter
As I very
Slowly settle
To the Bottom
Of the Mud.

And I find that
What a person
With a puddle
Round his middle
Thinks of mostly
In the muddle
Is the Muddi-
Ness of Mud.

Bigfoot

Bigfoot's sort of Blobby, so he can't exactly Walk,
And he sometimes doesn't answer, 'cause he does forget his Name,
And he likes to go to School, except he mainly eats the furniture —
    But Bigfoot's like a Terror,
    Bigfoot's like a Tiger,
    Bigfoot's tough as anything in Bad
                       Guy
                          Games!

Suppose that I'm pretending there's a Robber in the bedroom
And he's hiding in the closet, 'cause he knows I'd Mash him flat,
But he makes a mighty Charge, and he fights me to the window-sill —
    Then Bigfoot's like a Terror!
    Bigfoot's like a Tiger!
    Bigfoot's like a Lion in a Laun-
                        dro-
                           mat!

Or maybe I go out, and I'm being a Detective,
And I think I meet a Midget with a Long Black Veil,
But it isn't him at all, it's a Fat Ferocious Fighting-Freak —
    Then Bigfoot's like a Terror!
    Bigfoot's like a Tiger!
    Bigfoot's like a Jetplane with a Stinger
                        in its
                           Tail!

Bigfoot isn't Pretty, not unless you like the look of him.
Bigfoot isn't Clever, he can barely chew his gum.
But Bigfoot's always There, when there's Rotten kinds of Dangerous,
    And Bigfoot's like a Terror!
    Bigfoot's like a Tiger!
    Bigfoot always saves me, so he's Num-
                        ber
                           One!

Smelly Fred

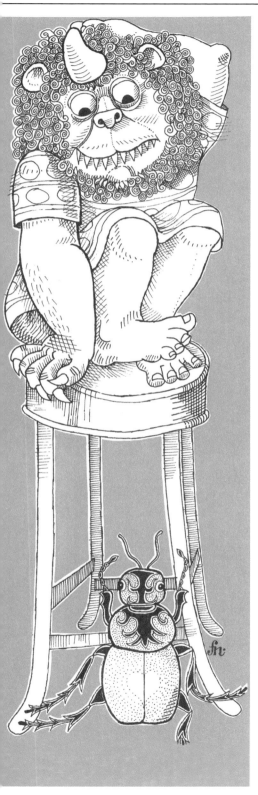

A sort of beetle-bug is crawling
    Up my running shoe;
His name is Smelly-Belly Fred
    But Smelly Fred will do.

And if he crawls across my shoe
    And starts to climb my sock,
I'm going to change his name, and call him
    Freddie-On-A-Walk,

'Cause with a name like that he'll want
    To climb on legs instead;
And then he'll climb up mine, and he'll be
    Skinny Winning Fred.

And Skinny Winning Fred will likely
    Want to try my shorts,
And there his name will change again
    To Freddo, King of Sports,

So then he'll get excited, and he'll
    Scamper up my top,
And we'll both shake hands, and cheer
               for grand
    Sir Frederick-Never-Stop!

And then there's only one thing left
    Before he's SUPER-FRED:
He has to crawl across my chin
    And balance on my head –

And when he does, I've got an extra
    Special thing to do! . . .
Darn it! Smelly Fred just tripped
    And tumbled off my shoe.

Goofy Song

Well I'm going down the road
And I look like a toad
    And I feel like Plasticine,
And the dust between my toes
Is like a tickle in my nose,
    But the puddles make them feel real clean —

    Hey!

And the hammer with the stammer
Is a dentist in disguise,
And the flyer on the wire
    Is a wren.
And the pizza that I'll eat's a
Little skimpy on the meat, so
I shall have to lay an egg
    Or eat a hen —

    Yo!

Now I'm going down the road
And I'll turn into a toad
    And I'll play with Plasticine.
And I don't know where I'm going
But I hope it isn't snowing
'Cause my underwear is showing
And the snow would start it growing
And my buddy's sure to throw it
    On my bean —

    Ee-yow!

Bike-Twister

Place a foot upon a pedal,
Put your pedal-pushers on;
To the pedal pin a paddle,
Paddle-pedal push upon.

Place the paddle-pedal-cycle
On a puddle in the park;
Paddle addled through the puddle,
Pump the pedal till it's dark.

On the puddle-pedal-paddler
Place a poodle with a pail:
Let the addled paddle-pedaller's
Puddle-poodle bail.

The Big Blue Frog and the Dirty Flannel Dog

Then the big
> blue
>> frog

And the dirty flannel dog
Said, "It's time to go to sea
On the good ship *Hollow Log.*"
First they sailed to Saskatoon,
Where they stole the harvest moon
> And they strung it as a headlight on the log.

Then they hitched
> their
>> pants

And they sailed away for France,
Roaring, "Pour a pint o' grog!"
As the waves began to dance.

But the North Wind with its spray
Blew them miles and miles away,
          And it smothered up the moon in mist and fog.

As they lay
                    upon
                              the beach
Sadly panting, each to each,
Deep-sea creatures came to sing
In a wet enchanted ring.
And they lit the moon again
And they leaped with might and main
          And they hung it in the heavens, glittering.

Then the moon
                    shone
                              bright
All the warm and blessèd night,
And they tore across the sand
Jigging high in pure delight.
And across the skipping sea
The silver light came washing free,
          And they bowed three times to that majestic sight.

Then the frog
          said,
                    "Friend,
Shall we sail on to the end,
Sail forever, straight ahead,
Far as light and sea extend?"
But the dog said, "No,
Much obliged – I don't think so."
          So they turned around,
                              and paddled home to bed.

I Eat Kids Yum Yum!

A child went out one day.
She only went to play.
A mighty monster came along
And sang its mighty monster song:

"I EAT KIDS YUM YUM!
I STUFF THEM DOWN MY TUM.
I ONLY LEAVE THE TEETH AND CLOTHES.
(I SPECIALLY LIKE THE TOES.)"

The child was not amused.
She stood there and refused.
Then with a skip and a little twirl
She sang the song of a hungry girl:

"I EAT MONSTERS BURP!
THEY MAKE ME SQUEAL AND SLURP.
IT'S TIME TO CHOMP AND TAKE A CHEW –
AND WHAT I'LL CHEW IS YOU!"

The monster ran like that!
It didn't stop to chat.
(The child went skipping home again
And ate her brother's model train.)

Garbage Delight

Now, I'm not the one
To say No to a bun,
And I always can manage some jelly;
If somebody gurgles,
"Please eat my hamburgles,"
I try to make room in my belly.
I seem, if they scream,
Not to gag on ice-cream,
And with fudge I can choke down my fright;
But none is enticing
Or even worth slicing,
Compared with Garbage Delight.

With a nip and a nibble
A drip and a dribble
A dollop, a walloping bite:
If you want to see grins
All the way to my shins,
Then give me some Garbage Delight!

I'm handy with candy.
I star with a bar.
And I'm known for my butterscotch burp;
I can stare in the eyes
Of a Toffee Surprise
And polish it off with one slurp.
My lick is the longest,
My chomp is the champ
And everyone envies my bite;
But my talents were wasted
Until I had tasted
The wonders of Garbage Delight.

With a nip and a nibble
A drip and a dribble
A dollop, a walloping bite:
If you want to see grins
All the way to my shins

Then give me some Garbage Delight,
Right now!
Please pass me the Garbage Delight.

The Snuggle Bunny

The snuggle bunny
　　Likes to scrunch
His body up
　　In a funny bunch

And wind his teddies
　　And his bears
Around and round
　　By their soft brown hairs,

And then he burrows
　　Like a mole
Inside the nearest
　　Snuggle hole

And he snoozles up
　　And he snozzles in,
And he goes to sleep
　　In his snuggle-down skin.

So if you stumble
　　Unawares
On a jumbly clutter
　　Of teddy bears,

Unzip the top
　　And sort and stir
Through soft brown layers
　　Of warm brown fur

And underneath,
　　With a faraway roar,
You'll hear a snuggled
　　Bunny snore.

"What Will You Be?"

They never stop asking me,
"What will you be? –
A doctor, a dancer,
A diver at sea?"

They never stop bugging me:
"What will you *be*?"
As if they expect me to
Stop being me.

When I grow up I'm going to be a Sneeze,
And sprinkle Germs on all my Enemies.

When I grow up I'm going to be a Toad,
And dump on Silly Questions in the road.

When I grow up, I'm going to be a Child.
I'll Play the whole darn day and drive them Wild.

The Operation

When you walk inside the kitchen
    Very kindly do not shout:
Poor old Hannah's getting mended
    'Cause her stuffing all came out.
There's a special dish of ice-cream
    And it's white and brown and red,
And there's cookies if we're quiet,
    'Cause we think it hurts her head.

And we never bash old Hannah
    On the floor, except today,
And my Mom has found her needle
    And she thinks she'll be OK;
And old Hannah's pretty brave, she's
    Trying not to cry or scream,
And I'm sorry that I done it
    And I'm having red ice-cream.

When you see the operation
    If you tiptoe you can watch,
'Cause her head is feeling better
    But she'll always have a blotch.
And be quiet when you look, and
    Very kindly mind her snout:
My old Hannah's pretty sick, because
    I pulled her stuffing out.

Well, I said I'm awful sorry
    And it wasn't nice to do,
And it might have been on accident
    Except that isn't true,
So I hope that she'll be friends again
    And let me play with her,
'Cause she's special to my mind, and now
    I'm going to comb her fur.

The Fly-Nest

I've got a sort of tying thing
    For when I have to tie,
And a box to be a fly-nest
    Cause I'm going to catch a fly.

But I don't exactly get it –
    How you get the fly inside:
Do you open up the lid a bit
    And just go off and hide?

'Cause a fly could come along, see,
    And he's looking for a nest,
But he doesn't understand, a box
    Is what a fly likes best.

So he marches up and tells me
    That a box was in the way,
And he rather liked the colour
    But he doesn't care to stay.

And suppose a bigger aminal
    Is walking with his kid,
And he spies a cozy fly-nest
    With a comfy sort of lid,

And they crawl inside, and then the nest
    Is full up to the brim –
And then the fly comes *back*, except
    There isn't room for him!

So I've got to get my tying stuff
    All ready for the plan:
I tell the fly to hurry
    Quick as anybody can,

And *before* those aminals go in
    We catch them round the chest,
And I keep them in my bedroom,
    And the fly can have his nest.

The Tiniest Man in the Washing Machine

The tiniest man
I've ever seen
Sleeps deep in a heap
In a washing machine.

At eight each night
He goes downstairs
And he yawns and puts on
The pyjamas he wears;

Then taking a bottle
From out of the sink,
He fixes a mixture
That's fizzy and pink,

And checking to see
That there's no one around,
He hops in the top
With a chugalug sound.

The buttons click,
The washer thuds,
And he wiggles and jiggles
In strawberry suds!

And around and around
He topples and flops,
A prince in a rinse
Till the cycle stops.

The foam is a pillow.
The pillow is deep.
He dreams of ice-cream
In a strawberry sleep

Till the morning comes up
And the sun comes up higher —
And he pops through the top,
Straight into the dryer,

And after he's shaken
The very last sud,
He roars out the door
And he rolls in the mud.

Beat Me and Bite Me

Beat me and bite me
    And teach me to bark,
I looked in the water
    And there saw the shark.

I looked in the shark,
    And it showed me its jaws.
And that is the reason
    I'm not, though I was.

Periwinkle Pizza

If you want to see a breakfast
Getting gobbled up and gone,
Give me periwinkle pizza
In the parlour in Saint John.

If you want to see a luncheon
Getting munched in seconds flat,
Give me periwinkle pizza
On a plate in Shediac.

If you want to see a supper
Getting shovelled into me,
Give me periwinkle pizza
In St. Andrews-by-the-Sea.

The Tickle Tiger

The tickle tiger
   Has a tail
Which she can flip
   And flick and flail

And tie into
   A figure 6
And swish, to snuff out
   Candle wicks,

And hang from with
   The greatest ease,
And use to tickle
   Enemies.

And if a person
   Plays a game,
Like calling her
   A rotten name,

Or roaring when
   She's not awake,
Or sitting on her
   By mistake,

She doesn't care
   To go about
And bop the person
   On the snout,

Or squish him with
   A red toboggan,
Or plant a pine tree
   On his noggin —

Instead she flicks
    Her tickle tail
Around and around
    Like a frisky whale

And with a whisk
    And a fidgety blink,
She leaves the person
    Tickled pink.

One day, a man
    Came by to steal
The tickle tiger
    For a meal;

He thought he'd have her
    For dessert,
With mustard (a dab),
    And ketchup (a squirt).

He set the table
    Neat and straight –
One knife, one fork,
    One spoon and plate –

And then invited
    Her to dinner,
Enquiring first
    If he could skin her.

The tickle tiger
    Didn't pause:
She stood up straight
    On her strong rear paws

And sharpened the tips
    Of her sharp sharp claws
And opened the jut
    Of her giant jaws

And then her tail
    Began to whirl
And swizzle and quiver
    And tingle and twirl –

And then, with no more
    Half-and-halfing,
She tickled his toes:
    The man died laughing.

The Pair of Pants

Johnny came from England
    Jackie came from France
They went to see a wise man
    About a pair of pants.

One said, "They're too long."
    One said, "They're too little."
The wise man took the pair of pants
    And ripped them up the middle.

Now each has got a pant-leg.
    Each is freezing, too.
And yet it seemed the only thing
    That anyone could do.

One Sunny Summer's Day

A Jersey cow exploded,
    One sunny summer's day.
The farmer was in Flin Flon,
    Combing his toupee.

The farmer's wife was farming,
    She didn't hear a thing.
(A motorist was injured
    And had to wear a sling.)

The Big Molice Pan and the Bertie Dumb

Once a big molice pan
    Met a Bertie Dumb,
Sitting on a wide sock
    Booing gubble chum.

"Hey," said the molice pan,
    "Gum and simmy come."
"Sot your rotten kicking pox!"
    Cried the Bertie Dumb.

Then the big molice pan
    Rank Jamaica drum,
Wide at dunce, but grows with runts.
    (Kate to strinkum. DUM.)

Bloody Bill

You say you want to fight me?
　　But you think I'd rather not?
Then listen to the story
　　Of another guy I fought,

And maybe you'll appreciate –
　　I don't like blood and dirt
All smudgy on my fingertips
　　And dripping down my skirt.

A famous pirate captain
　　By the name of Bloody Bill
Was marching up the sidewalk
　　On the old Spadina Hill.

He had a sort of eye-patch
　　That was caked and flaked in blood,
And he ground his teeth together
　　And he spat out bloody crud.

He wore a bloody dagger
　　In his muddy, bloody belt,
And on his back I saw the track
　　Of thirty bloody welts,

And then he slooshed his soggy boots
    Till blood ran down the hill;
I figured, by the look of things,
    It must be Bloody Bill.

And Bloody Bill was roaring drunk
    And Bloody Bill was loud
And Bloody Bill was picking fights
    With people in the crowd.

First I tried to walk around him
    Like a common passer-by;
I'm quite a gentle person
    And I wouldn't hurt a fly,

But Bloody Bill got wilder, like
    A bully and a crook,
And by the way, I meant to say
    He had a bloody hook.

He spied a frail old gentleman
    And seized him by the feet
And shook him upside-down until
    His change rolled in the street,

And then he pitched the gentleman
    Across a grotty sewer,
And no one had the nerve to speak
    Severely to the boor.

Now, I was out to buy some milk
    To take home to my Mum,
But I could see I'd have to teach
    Some manners to this bum

For pirates are a pleasure
    In the safety of a book,

But meeting one is much less fun,
    Especially with a hook.

And so I turned to face him,
    With a sigh of utter boredom,
And flicked my little finger, and
    Immediately floored him.

And holding back a yawn, I seized him
    By his smelly snout,
And I flipped his nose, and flicked his toes,
    And turned him inside out,

And wound him round a tree I found
    And beat with might and main,
Till all the booze and tobacco juice
    Had had a chance to drain.

(I know that bullies often come
    And boss around a kid.
But that's the way I do things:
    So that's the thing I did.)

I pelted him with melted cheese
    And fourteen devilled eggs;
I tied spaghetti to his hair,
    Lasagna to his legs,

And then, because I didn't like
    The way he'd used his fists,
I danced upon his ears, until
    He asked me to desist.

And when I turned him right-side-out
    He scuttled down the hill
And never once looked back at me –
    Just ran, did Bloody Bill.

And me, I washed my fingers
    Of the blood and scum and rum,
And bought a quart of two per cent
    And took it home to Mum.

So though I'd love to fight you,
    I am really very shy,
And leaving you all black and blue
    Would likely make me cry.

I don't *want* to turn you inside-out,
    Or wrap you round a tree:
Why don't you take your strong right thumb
    And suck it peacefully?

The Bratty Brother (Sister)

I dumped the bratty brother
In a shark-infested sea;
By dusk the sea was empty, and
The brat was home with me.

I mailed the bratty brother
To a jail in Moosonee;
The sobbing jailer mailed him back
The next day, C.O.D.

I wept, and hurled the bratty
Brother off the CN Tower;
He lolloped through the living room
In less than half an hour.

So now I keep my brother
In the furnace, nice and neat.
I can't wait till December
When my Dad turns on the heat.

The Bedtime Concert

It's a concert in the bedroom
    With the aminals and toys,
And they think they're making music
    So you mustn't call it noise:
Someone's beating on the bucket
    And he's beat it half to bits
And it's Drumming Monk McGonigle!
    I think he's lost his wits.

And old Hannah's got my trumpet,
    With the wrong end on her snout –
Every time she tries to blow, a sort of
    Sneezy sound comes out;
And the aminals keep playing
    Like as if they never guessed
That the concert in the bedroom
    Isn't what you call the best.

And old Bigfoot's got a whistle, and
    The whistle never stops,
So that every time it doesn't, I could
    Almost call the cops.
But the aminals keep marching
    And they must have marched a mile
And they're all of them so serious
    They make me want to smile.

It's a concert in the bedroom,
    It's a racket in my head,
And pretty soon I'll have to come
    And chase them off to bed.
But they're all my special Aminals,
    Though both my ears are sore,
So I guess I'll let them play for maybe
    Half a minute more.

Goofus

Sometimes my mind is crazy
Sometimes my mind is dumb
Sometimes it sings like angel wings
And beeps like kingdom come.

My mother calls me Mary
My father calls me Fred
My brother calls me Stumblebum
And kicks me out of bed.

Go tell it on a T-shirt
Go tell a TV screen:
My summy's turning tummersaults
And I am turning green.

Don't come to me in April
    Don't come to me in Guelph
Don't come to me in anything
    Except your crummy self.

I haven't got a dollar
    I haven't got a dime
I haven't got a thing to do
    But write these goofy rhymes.

Sometimes my mind is crazy
    Sometimes my mind is dumb
Sometimes it sings like angel wings
    And beeps like kingdom come.

The Secret Song

I've got a secret
    Song I sing
That's secret and special
    As anything.

It's sort of a magical
    Whispery fizz,
But I'm never quite sure
    What the tune part is —

So I jump ahead
    From the stop at the start
To the squeak at the very
    Ending part

Which is actually more
    Of a whistling and dinning,
And everyone thinks
    That it's still the beginning.

And I'm never quite sure
    How the words of it go,
But I just leave them out
    And they don't even show.

And it always works,
    And nobody knows
How my magical, secret
    Sing-song goes.